Knowing Horses by Heart

Knowing Horses by Heart

A Collection of Poems Written with Appreciation for the Horses in My World

Barbara J. Hutson

iUniverse, Inc.
Bloomington

Knowing Horses by Heart
A Collection of Poems Written with Appreciation
for the Horses in My World

Correspondence or comments to author can be made at barbarahutson@windstream.net

iUniverse books may be ordered through booksellers or by contacting:

iUniverse
1663 Liberty Drive
Bloomington, IN 47403
www.iuniverse.com
1-800-Authors (1-800-288-4677)

Illustrations are by renown international artist, Sylva Alana Timiniskis. To those "in the know" of the art world, she is recognized on a first name basis—"Sylva". It is her unconditional dedication and loyalty to our friendship that served as her inspiration. Her efforts, along with her husband, Bill Timinskis' finishing touches and formatting are the icing on the proverbial cake—delicious. View Sylva's art at http://sylvaart.com

ISBN: 978-1-4759-3919-4 (sc)
ISBN: 978-1-4759-3918-7 (hc)
ISBN: 978-1-4759-3920-0 (e)

Printed in the United States of America

iUniverse rev. date: 07/23/2012

Dedicated to those wonderful people who never stop searching for a better and kinder way with horses - you know who you are. ♥

Horses - My Magnificent Obsession

{ Table of Contents }

{ Acknowledgements }

A heartfelt thank you to my friends and family who have indulged me in my lifelong love affair with horses.

A huge hug to my tolerant and wonderful husband, Byron, for understanding how deeply I feel about horses and for supporting me - even if he doesn't get it.

An especially warm feeling goes to my dear friend and business partner, Julia, for being a rare like-minded soul whom I can share my thoughts and experiences concerning horses with.

I am particularly grateful for the illustrations that my dear friend, Sylva brought forth from simple photographs of my horses. Her expertise and professionalism is obvious in her depictions and the way she captures the sentiment of the related poems is uncanny. Her input puts a polish on Knowing Horses by Heart that I wouldn't have had without her. Much the same way being her friend has put a shine on my life.

My absolute gratitude goes to that Greater Power that brought such magnificent creatures into existence and into my world—making it an infinitely better place.

And, of course, my deep appreciation for the horses who have filled my dreams since childhood and continue to do so.

{ Introduction }

I fell in love with horses. I don't remember how or when it happened. There was no defining moment when I laid eyes on them for the first time and my life was changed. Since before I can remember, I have been under their spell. I believe I came into this world loving horses. I seem to have recognized them from some spiritual realm, even as an infant.

This love I "fell in" has been like a huge abyss of infatuation, admiration and intrigue of which I have been adrift on to varying degrees for my entire life. At times, I was in over my head, totally immersing myself in their essence. Other times I was just wading in around the shallow edges longing to plunge in but being held back by life's circumstances. The interest was always there, just below the surface, waiting to emerge. Loving horses has been the single constant in over 60 years of a lifetime filled with change, confusion, growth and evolving perspectives.

This world is full of spectacular and fascinating wonders just waiting to be discovered and experienced. I have never found anything that captivates me as totally as the spirit of horses. They are the embodiment of the ultimate gift given to humans reminding us that there is no limit to the beautiful and wonderful creations our Source is capable of manifesting and willing to share with us.

{ A Ride in the Snow }

I walked down the hill to the barn where my horses are found
On a clear winter's morning with fresh snow on the ground

I heard the soft nickers greeting me from the stalls
I saw the halters all hanging from the hooks on the walls

I made up a warm mash to chase off the chill
And stood listening to them eating as hungry horses will

I really had no intention of riding that day
Just doing my chores then going my way

I suddenly felt an old memory deep inside of me stir
Was it really so wonderful? I had to be sure

I walked over to the stall where my favorite mare stood
And right then and there decided I would

When she had finished her breakfast and her belly was full
I snapped on her lead rope and gently gave it a pull

I saddled her up and we headed on out
Feeling that it is times like this are what it's about

Just me and my horse the world silent and white
Quietly trotting out to meet the day's first light

She was tossing her head and wanting to go
Excited to be travelling on the year's first snow

At first I was worried, afraid she would slip
But she told me in her way, she was up for the trip

So, I loosened the reins and away we did fly
I couldn't have stopped her - I didn't try

The snow was flying and the sky turning blue
When I realized this ride belonged to her too

I knew she was having even more fun than me
We both felt the thrill you feel being free

Her mane was blowing back as she kicked up her heels
I knew she was remembering how a young filly feels

The reason I know what I'm saying is true
Is because I was feeling like a young girl too

It had been a very long time, a good many years
Since I had turned it all loose, put away all my fears

I trusted her to carry me safely that day
To the place deep inside me where old memories lay

To a time I was young, carefree and bold
Before I turned 50, before she was sold

Back to a time when my very first horse and me
Ran alone in the snow with me laughing with glee

It all came back to me on that morning ride
Tears of a pure youthful joy I could no longer hide

I slowed my horse down and as we wandered along
The crunch of the snow played out like a song

There's nothing else like it, no music so sweet
As the rhythm beat out by my mare's four feet

Add to the mix my dog running happily astride
I felt the grin on my face stretching ever so wide

When it was over and I quietly walked at her side
I silently thanked her again for the wonderful ride

I gave her an apple for the new memory I'll keep
I buried my face in her neck and breathed in deep

There's no better smell anywhere on this earth
There's no way to explain just what it is worth

I turned her loose and away up the hill she did run
Glistening and golden in the mid-morning sun

It's a magical thing, a treasure I know
To have such vivid memories of a ride in the snow

{ Aromatherapy }

You may think me crazy
And that may be true
But one of my favorite smells
Just may surprise you

It's not the heady aroma
That comes from the flowers
That fills up the air
After warm spring showers

It is not exotic perfumes
Rich potpourri or spice
Those aren't the things
That make me sniff twice

It's not fresh bread baking
Although, it comes close
I will tell you what scent
I love the most

It's when I bury my face
In my horse's neck
That makes me all giddy
That makes me a wreck

I can't explain just what
That smell does to me
But it makes my heart skip
And it fills me with glee

So warm and so earthy
I know of nothing so good
I would bottle and sell it
If only I could

I take deep breaths
I just can't get enough
I don't know why, but
I love that stuff

Maybe it's because it
Makes it all real
I have a horse
How lucky I feel

Maybe it's because
I go to a place in my mind
Where the best things are kept
Things only I can find

Or maybe it's because
Dreams get buried in sleep
They only can reach me
When I breathe her scent deep

Of all of my treasures
This is one I won't trade
This is one I shall value
It's worth doesn't fade

If you have never experienced
What I am talking about
Make it a point in your life
And don't go without

Close your eyes tight
And get up real close
Press into her neck
With the end of your nose

Let the scent take you
Into the world of horses
Away with the wind
And all nature's forces

I hope you will feel the power
When you take in the smell
But if you don't understand it
It is a secret I'll never tell

{ Ask a Mare }

Unlike the obliging gelding
That wants or needs to be told
What you need from him next—
Be soft and quiet or fast and bold

He willingly heeds your commands
With no qualms or questions in mind
He's known to be trusting and obedient
The predicable push-button kind

Or the magnificent stallion who demands
The right to an equal vote in the matter
Regardless of the time or subject at hand
Dismissing direct orders and useless chatter

The only real way he will ever be convinced
To accept your challenge or grant an appeal
Is with a confident horse-to-man discussion
In what may end up being a lengthy ordeal

When it comes to the more feminine gender
I can tell you what's true on any given day
A mare needs you to give her opinion a chance
Let her be heard, let her have her say

To get her to give her best performance
And be the great girl you've come to expect
Avoid giving orders in a no-nonsense way
Remember she's female and show her respect

Don't use a strong hand to bully her,
Show her who's boss, or force her along
She'll tune you out or maybe even resist
If she's uneasy or if she thinks you are wrong

If she's the Alpha who looks out for the herd
Remember her position and please don't forget
She carries the responsibility of her job seriously
She won't hesitate to offer her life to protect

Like a typical, multi-facetted woman
Her work and her day is never done
She perpetually keeps watch over her charges
And when you're around, even considers you one

And that is the reason nothing is taken for granted
There is a lot on her plate and she needs to be sure
She doesn't mean to be trying, stubborn or moody
She has to be careful - her reasons are pure

Times when she balks or questions your asking
Sidesteps restlessly and throws nervous glances
Just stay calm, don't be angry and impatient
Understand while she heeds her mind's dances

A mare's self-preservation runs extremely high
It is those basest of instincts that make her the best
Give her the time and the chance to determine
When she feels it's OK to grant your request

When it comes to generalities and common cliché's
I admit I have enjoyed giving and getting my share
I get protective when it comes to sayings about horses
Because not a whole lot of truth is usually found there

But with this particular quote about my equine friends
I have to say, I believe the assessment is mostly fair
"You may tell a gelding & discuss it with a stallion,
But always remember it's best to kindly *ask* a mare"

{ Barnyard Glamour }

When it comes up in conversation
That my job is running a stable
I will get the most envious looks
Like my life is somewhat of a fable

"You're living my dream"
I've heard it over and over
As they envision beautiful horses
Grazing in grassy fields with clover

They imagine and ponder
And how great it must be
How romantic and thrilling
To be around horses like me

The soft nickers and nuzzles
The majestic beauty and speed
The private comical antics
Are an envious treasure indeed

And while those things may be true
And I love it with all of my heart
They are missing my life's daily reality
What I call the "glamorous" part

To them, an occasional trip to the barn
Is exciting and their eyes gleam with stars
But the first thing I notice upon their arrival
Is them on a cell phone in their clean spiffy cars

You see, what serves as my "limo"
Rides smooth as a buck
Better known to us horse people
As simply "the truck"

The outside is usually dusty
And sometimes covered in mud
The interior littered with horse stuff
Along with dog hair and crud

As far as the luxury of using a phone
It isn't a practical or a wise thing for me
To let my attention wander elsewhere
Let alone the use my hands not being free

The visitors come to look at the horses
Dressed in immaculately clean clothes
Carefully trying not to get anything icky
On all those cute ruffles, ribbons and bows

The wearing of those fine clothes
May be most every girl's wish
But when it comes to the barnyard
I think my old jeans are more stylish

The ladies' hair may be coiffed
And I know what they pay
While my extensions are free
And consist of pieces of hay

To them, messed up hair like mine
Is considered almost a crime
Simply caught in a ponytail
Almost all of the time

Their nails are just perfect
Neatly manicured and clean
While mine are more "natural"
You know what I mean?

They come wearing cute sandals
Or shiny boots without even a scuff
Compared to my trusty barn shoes
Broke in, dirty, faded and rough

They are adorned in necklaces
And dangling gold earrings
My jewelry hangs over my shoulder
Like ropes, halters and things

The pampered girls have hands
So soft, dainty, and smooth
Mine are more like the leather
No amount of lotion can soothe

Their workout routines are done
On fancy machines and ballet rails
I get my daily exercise with
A pitchfork and by carrying pails

They take so much time
To make up their faces just so
While I jump out of bed and
Straight to the barn I do go

When nature comes calling
And there is a need for relief
A suggested trip behind the barn
Brings looks of disbelief

I wonder if they would wish
To give my life a try
When I am soaked in the rain
And they are inside and dry

How many would really
Trade places with me
And choose to be sweating
When it is 100 degrees?

If given the choice,
Would their dreams be true?
Would they really and honestly
Want to do what I do?

Would they truly give up
The comforts they've known
To take on the "good life"
If the reality was shown?

That is why I inwardly grin
When I hear women say
"You are living my dream"
And I know I am, - in my way

Although barnyard glamour is iffy,
The choice I made remains clear
For there is no other place on this earth
That holds my heart so dear

Maybe my life isn't all that desirable
As it is imagined by others to be
But I would never forsake it
It is the perfect lifestyle for me

{ Birth of a Foal }

There is just no explaining the extent of the thrill
Of expecting the arrival of a newborn foal
Just waiting and watching in the midnight chill
Staying steady and ready being my primary role

My mare's been uneasy and pacing most of the night
So I settle in to bunk just outside of her stall
I don't want to bother her so I stay out of sight
Knowing that if she needs me, I won't miss her call

Her pacing increases and she breaks into a sweat
I try to peek over the stall door quiet and still
She seems ready but her glance tells me no, not yet
Everything will be fine. I just pray that it will

So I go back to my bed to give her some space
Thinking I am probably just making her anxious
She needs to go through this at her own natural pace
She doesn't need me nervously making a fuss

I must have dozed off for an hour or so
Because I woke with a start and my heart froze
I could no longer hear her pacing to and fro
So I run to the stall while my panic grows

I shine the flashlight into the dark space
She's standing quietly eating away at the hay
Then my light finds the most wondrous face
Of my new foal staring at me from where he lay

My heart stood still and my breath escaped me
As I looked at this perfectly beautiful being
This was truly a miracle, I know you'd agree
Even I could hardly believe what I was seeing

A big white blaze shone bright as the moon
Lighting up his face as he took in his new world
Then as I watched what seemed to be way too soon
He tried to stand and those long legs unfurled

With soft nudges of encouragement from his mother
It wasn't long at all before he was up on his feet
I held perfectly still until I thought I would smother
Exhaling only when he successfully found her full teat

The emotion grew until I was sure my heart would burst
Watching those first minutes of my dream come true
I grabbed my phone and knew just who I would call first
I need my best friend there with me to witness this too

Those first wobbly steps grew ever steady and stronger
And he was actually running around in a very short time
Then he grew sleepy and just couldn't go any longer
I watched him napping and couldn't believe he was mine

Years have gone by now and held so many wondrous ways
Hardly a day has gone by that he has not been in my sight
He is one of life's greatest gifts and brightens my days
But nothing compares to how I felt on that magical night

Built for Comfort, Not for Speed

My recent riding style has taken a turn
I am much more mellow and laid back now
As I grow older and, I hope, much wiser
I find I enjoy the "why" more than the how

My seat seeks out comfort while strolling along
I like to relax and just rock with the beat
To take in the natural wonders surrounding me
Being aware of the rhythm of my horse's feet

I savor those peaceful moments spent
When the rest of the world drifts away
As me and my horse amble along on the trails
Time passes serenely - nothing to say

These days there are rarely wild shouts
Of "Giddy Up!", "Yahoo!" and "Yippee!"
The expressions are more like gentle nudges
Quietly exchanged between my steed and me

I was much different when I was younger
Indeed, it was an altogether different story
I craved the speed and feeling of power
I knew no fear. It was all guts and all glory

I lived for those thrilling times on my horse
When off like a whirlwind we would go
Rapidly covering fields and county roads
Neither Blaze nor I saw any need to go slow

Planning a ride based around perfect weather
Was never an option, factor or goal
Together we raced through it all
Summer's heat, the rain and the snow

Now if the forecast is not fairly decent
And the temperature promising to be mild
I find myself making up excuses and reasons
Painfully aware that I am no longer a child

I still thoroughly enjoy riding my horses
If possible, maybe even more than before
The difference is I try a lot harder now to avoid
Activities that cause bruises or make me sore

With age comes changes in so many aspects
And I'm not speaking of only the obvious physical
My thinking also tends to be slowed down some
I find myself happily turning more to the whimsical

Now, instead of being in a hectic and constant rush
And having the need to feel the wind grabbing my hair
I spend more time dwelling in that peaceful state
I can only find alone when my horse carries me there

I am not saying all those fast and furious days are past
That on occasion I won't be feeling the need
I am just saying that I am finding more here lately
That I am built more for comfort than for speed

{ Equi-Accidents }

We've heard many a story
About taking a great fall
From riding a fast horse
No matter how big or how small

We've gotten the warnings
Of walking behind a strange horse
Of the kicks you may get
Delivered with power and force

We've all been told
But can't seem to quit
Feeding snacks from your hand
May cause you to get bit

Broken bones happen quickly
And take time to heal
I am not discounting the stories-
I know they are real

There is some truth in these warnings
And these things may occur rarely
But the real hazards of horses
Come from what happens daily

Now I am not stating the obvious
Like a fall, kick or a buck
Just everyday slip ups
Or just a run of bad luck

It's the little unnoticed things
That seem to always add up
That proves our commitment
That fills up our cup

Hands and faces get chapped
The work never gets through
The everyday chores
Can get the better of you

There are no signals
No warnings spoken
To tell you about the many
Toes that get broken

Getting your foot stepped on
Is all in a day's work
Of working with horses
Consider it one of the perks

How about the bruised knee-caps
From getting too close to the fence
The reasons you are limping
From that day hence

Ever had your face slapped
From a low-hanging tree?
I am here to tell you
It has happened to me

Then there are the rope burns
On many a hand
When a horse leaps forward
And you take a stand

Splinters have been plucked
From arms leaning on a wood rail
Many a pinch on the fingers
Caused by carrying a pail

Scraped knuckles are normal
Band aids always available
You can't be without them
When running a stable

I've had my fair share
Of a black eye or two
From a horse slinging her head
While just passing through

Beware of the stall doors
Or the gates that have latches
Fingers get smashed there
On top of the scratches

And while at the gate
Be sure and take note
Bees are just waiting
To give you a poke

Who hasn't been hit with a buckle
While slinging a coat or a sheet
Over the back of a horse
To ward off the rain and the sleet?

Speaking of rain,
How about falling in mud
While leading a horse
Just after a flood?

Here's one of my favorites
I don't suppose
You've ever given a bath
And tripped over the hose

Thumbs have been known
To get in the way
Of hammers mending fences
And trailer hitches that stray

Fingernails are broken
Tightening a cinch
Not even worth mentioning
The occasional pinch

I've got a dent on my shin
Caused by my failure
To look out for that hitch thing
Where I hook up the trailer

Then there's the torment
Of those pesky flies
Buzzing around you
While you work at the ties

A single wrong movement
A turn or a twist
Can conjure up a sprain
Of an ankle or wrist

A tender spot on my hip
Has me searching for clues
To explain how I got
That big purple bruise

There is a scar left behind
Where they took off a lump
Just under my ribcage
From a saddle horn bump

Sometimes I wonder
If it's my lack of grace
That causes me to get
An occasional tail in the face

Breaking up ice in water buckets
Causes fingers to freeze
Heat in the summer months
Has you begging for a breeze

Have you ever been knocked over
By a horse when she shied
Or had your heart broken
By a horse when he died?

These are the real hazards
The constant that forces
Us to look at our life
Of working with horses

Not counting my injuries
I know there have been many
I would be rich now
If each one were a penny

It must be a sickness
For me there's no cure
And that is only a sampling
Of what I endure

But for all of the trouble
And all of the pain
If I had it to do over
I would do it again

Anything worth having
Comes at a cost
I can't think of the hurt
Or the blood that I've lost

You see, the injuries are
A small price to pay
For the joy of being with horses
Because my work is my play

That being said
I can't stress it enough
If you're gonna be around horses
You've gotta be tough.

{ Folk Remedy }

Folk lore has a well-known remedy
Used if you have been drinking too much
Commonly called "Hair of the Dog"
Which claims to cure nasty hangovers and such

Knowledge of the success rate it boasts of
Got me to seriously thinking-
Why not apply this same reasoning
To episodes other than drinking?

I sat and thought quite a bit about it
And eventually concluded "Of Course!"
The very same method will surely work
If applied to problems regarding my horse

We all know there is no better way
To get yourself over a really bad fall
Than to get back up on that same horse
And forget that it ever happened at all

Calmly taking a leap on a trail
Over a random, harmless old stump
Makes you forget how nervous you were
As you were approaching a failed jump

Because you've practiced it over and over
Your friend can now easily walk slow and lazy
Past those feared imaginary horse-eating monsters
That once used to make your equine act crazy

I know of no other good way to address
The scare of surviving a run-away
Than leisurely taking a nice quiet ride
That is the single most proven way

There is absolutely no substitution
To cure the unfortunate broken hearted
Than acquiring another horse to love
Once your four legged friend has departed

I, for one, can attest by knowing first hand
Just how magical and healing they can be
When I learned through my own experience
How well this works when they helped me

After weeks of nursing my poor broken ankle
One hand on the fence kept me propped up
While I happily brushed my favorite gelding
Discovering the therapy I needed so much

It was also my trusty older mare's shoulder
That patiently bore my unsteady weight
While taking my first steps without crutches
After that traumatic injury sealed my fate

Although that particular incident happened
From an occurrence related to riding a horse
I instinctively knew that they were the key
To making me whole and getting on course

Those bittersweet visits I made to the barn
Filled empty hours with the essence they emit
Kept up my spirits and me looking forward
Never allowing me any reason or option to quit

If a tainted experience with horses
Has caused you to endure fear or pain
The best cure is a dose of this remedy
Which means getting back with them again

It may be true that horse people are crazy
Many others believe it, of that I'm sure
We seem to have some strange addiction
With no interest to change and only horses cure

So you see there really is some wisdom
And that old folk lore is obviously true
The best remedy of all is "hair of the horse"
Give yourself another shot of what ails you

{ Hanging Out }

Sometimes when I'm having one of those days
When I find myself restless and all alone
I don't feel like cleaning or reading a book
The last thing I want is to talk on the phone

There is one sure way guaranteed to lift my spirits
I walk out to where my horses are hanging around
Quietly grazing, snoozing or playing together
And sit down to watch from there on the ground

In just a few moments, the energy shifts to me
As curiosity makes them lift their heads and stare
A glance passes between them as if discussing it
Wondering what is up now and why am I there?

They know it is not time to come in for dinner
And I am not approaching with a halter in hand
They can tell I'm not thinking about wanting to ride
Expressions are comical as they try to understand

It doesn't take long before they start coming my way
At first slow and cautiously in case it's a trick
They watch my Alpha mare for the "it's OK" signal
And when she gives the nod, the pace gets quick

All of a sudden on approaching they break into a run
And I literally feel the earth beneath me shake
The rumble of their hooves fills my ears like thunder
As I sit there wondering if this isn't a mistake

Thoughts that I should probably get out of the way
Come too late and there is no place to run if I could
So I sit quietly not speaking or moving a muscle
As they surround me as only a herd of horses would

And then the most magical moments begin to unfold
When my trust in them pays off right there in the field
They don't trample me or even think that they could
They suddenly stop and their kind hearts are revealed

At first they all check to be sure I am not carrying treats
Their noses explore my pockets as they tower above me
The experience is humbling looking at horses from this angle
Their huge feet are intimidating from the view that I see

As the realization sets in that we are amongst friends
Doubts between us fade and the question of motive resolved
Shortly they return their attention to the endless task of eating
It's a comfortable silence - any tensions between us dissolved

The next hour or so is spent in just observing my horses
We don't have to interact – I know they know I am there
They give me brief glimpses into life of their private world
I savor the moments and deeply appreciate what they share

They pay me the ultimate compliment by staying close by
Letting me know they don't mind me remaining so near
It is an honor I treasure and don't take lightly because
When I am alone with my horses I have nothing to fear

Needless to say, when I leave my attitude is brighter
Than before I "wasted" my day just doing nothing
I have no great remedies or solutions for problems
I can't explain what - only that I learned something

That "something" I take with me after my visits
Makes me take stock of my life, in fact it forces
Me to appreciate my days and count all my blessings
Which add up quickly when counting twice for my horses

{ Horsework before Housework }

I wake up in the morning
My intentions are good
I look around me
I know that I should
Start cleaning the house
Dusting off all the wood
It really needs doing
If only I could

But the horses are hungry
The chores must come first
I'll just get them done quickly
I vow with a curse
It may be lunchtime
If worst comes to worst
I am determined to do it
My lips are pursed

"I am off to the barn"
I call as I go out the door
I can't help but notice
The dirt on the floor
There's dishes and laundry
The bills and then more
I dread doing housework
I find it a bore

I get to the barn
And start putting out feed
I fill all the buckets
With water they'll need
I gather the halters
So that I can lead
The horses to eat
And get back to the deed

I've got to hurry
I've got to get done
I'm thinking I can finish
By noon or by one
Then the feeling comes on
I am powerless to shun
I just start having
Way too much fun

The horses are munching
Their feed and the hay
I love to just watch them
What can I say?
I think that if I am quick
I can squeeze in some play
That's when it starts
There goes my day

I walk over to fill
The large watering tub
That's when I notice
It could use a good scrub
So I grab up a brush

And busily scour and rub
Thinking I should be home
Cleaning my own sink and my tub

Back to the barn
To clean up the mess
I have plenty time
I think more or less
To get to the housework
The list seems so endless
That my mind starts to wander
And then I regress

I look at the horses
I think of the tack
That needs a good oiling
Before the next hack
So I get out a rag
And start losing track
Of when to stop doing
And when to get back

By now the horses are ready
But that's when I see
They could use a good brushing
It's all up to me
So we walk on over to stand
In the shade of the tree
Where I groom each one
Until they shine like the sea

But I am still not happy
So I hook up the hose
I start running the water
Over the dirt on their toes
White feet get dirty
A horse owner knows
By now I have water
On my boots and my clothes

I go back to the house to get
Dry socks for my feet
When the clock strikes noon
And now it's time to eat
So I fix some lunch
And grab me a seat
Aware time's running out
So I quicken my beat

I head back to the barn
And tackle the stalls
I sweep down the cobwebs
From the corners and walls
All the while blocking signals
My nonstop mind recalls
I've got to do housework
I know duty calls

I am almost there
Just one more thing
I need to pick out
The pens and the ring
I go to work

I am starting to sing
As I work my way through
The muck that I sling

I am getting close now
I think I'm through
When the dogs come running
Up out of the blue
They are smelling real bad
So what else can I do
But give them a bath
And wash off the goo

Finally I'm ready
To head back inside
Back to clean house
When a car pulls along side
My friend sticks her head out
And I swear that I tried
But I couldn't resist
When she asked me to ride

So we saddled the horses
There was guilt in my heart
But not strong enough to keep
Me from taking a part
Maybe it was unnecessary
Riding was not on the chart
I know that I sure enjoyed it
Even knowing it was not smart

Now dusk is coming
And it's getting late
I still haven't got to
The job that I hate
I know it's still there
But it will just have to wait
Because the evening chores
Are now on my plate

It is almost dark now
And I am tired and worn
I am happy and hungry
As the day I was born
I have to admit that
I am not really torn
By that nagging feeling
In my side like a thorn

I'll get to it tomorrow
I will even do more
I will clean all the windows
And even the scores
I promise my husband
I'll give it what for
Just as soon as I'm finished
Doing the chores

{ Little Girl Giggles }

The gift is sweeter than that very first kiss
Seeing those looks of sheer wonder and bliss
There is nothing quite like watching the eyes
Of a child as she squeals with excited cries
As the magic of real horses fills up the space
The look of pure amazement covers her face

Sure, there had been pictures seen in a book
And countryside car rides had provided a look
But nothing prepared her for standing by the real thing
She had no idea how they would make her heart sing
Although they appeared huge when being so near
Not for one moment did her thoughts turn to fear

This was the moment she had been dreaming of
Her chance to actually experience her vision of love
As she reaches her hand to touch that velvety nose
The grin on her face tells me she already knows
About that special world where fantasies stream
Of having a horse of her own – a little girls dream

How many times has she thought of moments like these?
How many bedtimes prayers had she said on her knees?
Feeling the anguish of an impossible, forbidden love
Believing and seeking an answer from God up above
Begging for a chance to prove her heart was true
How much she would care and the chores she would do

But right at this moment she forgets her grudge
And she lets out a giggle when she gets a nudge
There is a horse there beside her waiting to see
Just what this friendly visit would turn out to be
The moment of truth has finally arrived
The horse was saddled and she can go for a ride

The horse is so big and the girl's heart was bared
Was she really that brave or would she be scared?
This is what she thought she had wanted for so very long
But I saw her lower lip quiver as she tried to be strong
She was lifted up onto the saddle across its' strong back
I picked up the lead line and took up the slack

As the horse took a step forward I was so very proud
When the little girl started to laugh right out loud
It was hard to contain the overwhelming joy we got
Hearing her giggles when bouncing along at a trot
She had conquered her fears and savored the thrill
Of a gift that can be gotten as only riding a horse will

It is these times that continue to give me such pleasure
It is the life's lessons horses teach us that I so treasure
Such an array of extreme emotions, so many choices
Dreams and fears are real here and more than just voices
That little girl was changed by that horse that day
I have seen it done again and again – it is their way

{ Poetry in Motion }

There is more to having horses
Than riding I've found
It's more about how they look
The feel and the sound
Sometimes I'll stand there
Or sit on the ground
Watching my horses grazing
And milling around

There is something about it
Somewhere I read
About looking at horses
One famous man said
It's good for a man's soul
It clears out his head
I can attest to its truth
Look at the life I have led

For when I am around horses
I have to say
My troubles all vanish and
The world goes away
Nothing else matters
And my thoughts stray
Just watching my horses
Making my day

I can't help but marvel
At the beauty and grace
The perfection of movement
We humans chase
It's the look in their eyes
On such a beautiful face
That catches our breath
And makes our hearts race

It doesn't matter whether
They are moving or still
Holding them in my vision
Always gives me a thrill
Such amazing creatures
Made of spirit and will
There is a place in my heart
Only horses can fill

{ The Art of Saying Goodbye }

No more can be done to help your horse
Now that dreadful day has come along
When you must muster your strength
And dig deep inside so you can be strong

There's no need for more discussion
The final decision has been made
There is no more hoping and praying
There are no more barters or trade

This isn't the way he would choose to live
And you can't watch him go on this way
With a heavy heart you call in to the vet
Knowing your horse will be gone after today

You spend these last hours right by his side
Watching the clock as the minutes tick by
Trying to take in all the things you will miss
Embedding in memory his beautiful eye

You watch as the truck turns into the drive
You get the scissors and cut a lock of his mane
While the vet prepares the needle that will end his life
You know that it's the right thing ending his pain

His place has been chosen and is ready for him
A beautiful clearing at the edge of the wood
He will be close to his barn and all of his buddies
You prepare yourself now as best as you could

The hole has been dug where he will be laid
And you lead him over to what will be his grave
He walks along side you on unsteady legs
But he is calm and quiet. He is so brave

One last kiss before you give the nod
Stay with him as he drops and slips away
You are the last thing he sees, his trust is in you
The ultimate price of that hurt you willingly pay

Now that it's over and you are sure that he's gone
Your beloved horse lying so still on the ground
You gently place his coat to cover his head
Even the dogs are silent as they gather around

Before they bury him you take one last look
Making sure he has everything he will want or need
To make that trip over the rainbow bridge
To the place horses go when their soul is freed

Even now as I relive these moving moments
Hot tears will come and spill from my eyes
The hole in my heart has never been healed
Even though it's been years since we said our goodbyes

He comes to me some nights still if I'm lucky
I search for him while I am lost deep in my dreams
My heart wants to burst as he runs up to greet me
He's waiting for me on the other side it seems

I have to believe that I will be with him again
When I leave this earth, when I should die
I will meet up with my horse and take that last ride
Only this time we'll be flying together across the sky

{ Tough Choices }

The day is a glorious one and I have set it aside
To spend it with my horses and go for a ride
I pull on my jeans, lace my boots and tie up my hair
Head down to the pasture because my horses are there
I breathe in the fresh air and feel the sun on my face
Aware of my blessings as excitement quickens my pace

As I draw nearer the barn the reality of my dilemma sets in
Although I know that whatever I decide, I will still win
I have an ongoing problem I deal with on a regular basis
That pops up whenever I see all five of my horses' faces
There is just not enough time in the day or energy in me
To divide my attention into portions distributed equally

So while it's a great problem, they are still tough choices
Deciding the best way to go about quieting these inner voices
There is not a favorite that automatically comes to my mind
Besides, choosing that way wouldn't be either fair nor kind
Each one has its unique gift given so sweetly and freely to me
And each has its need for improvement so that we can agree

It is hard to explain how my itinerary is ultimately made
There is a certain rotation to be sure a foundation is laid
Sometimes there's a mission that gives it a priority status
Other times it's loneliness for a horse that gives it free gratis
It could be as simple as the kind of mood I am in that day
That will dictate how I spend my time and with whom I play

My older mare always needs exercise to keep her young and agile
I couldn't bear to think my lack of doing could make her fragile
If the truth be known it is me who will benefit the most from her
No matter what other troubles I might have, she is my cure
Like a pair of worn out favorite broken-in shoes
A few minutes on Guilty and gone are my blues

Then there is Cruise, my handsome slightly higher strung black
Who just can't seem to settle while I'm on his back
He needs more miles and hours to soften his yield to the touch
But his accident-prone traits keep that from happening much
He can be a bit of a challenge and is more than eager to go
My goal is to let him know it is OK to just take it slow

I am starting a youngster and there is a whole world to conquer
It's a constant trial and error finding methods we both prefer
Everyday handling wouldn't be too much even if it were possible
So I try to get in every minute to make his success more probable
My beautiful paint gelding is like a blank canvas awaiting the brush
My plan is to dedicate plenty of time and not give him the rush

Dixie's markings are brilliant and just the sight of her a delight
She looks out for her boy while awaiting her turn in the spotlight
She speaks with quiet murmurs when she sees me approaching
And gives her heart openly when the subject of trust is broaching
I need to maintain that bond between us that took so long to build
I give her thanks everyday for the void that she filled

Ah yes, then there is my gifted, gorgeous and most perfect Breeze,
Who makes having a horse look like a job done with such ease
The problem lies in the fact that he doesn't seem to need me at all
He doesn't seek my attention and is content left alone in his stall

He doesn't need any fine tuning and always performs his job well
I have to make it a point not to take him for granted for being so swell

Thank goodness making the really tough choices is not done everyday
Ones like having to choose who will go and which ones will stay
Like having to decide between one and another when trying to buy
And seeing the time run out and determining the time to let them die
Or establishing a level of involvement I might wish to take
To help a horse get over some human's insensitive training mistake

I have a hard enough time deciding how to spend my next few hours
Even knowing that there is no ambush of evil, mystical powers
Knowing full well it will be wonderful whichever horse I choose
I still struggle with it even though there is no way I can lose
"That is silly" you might say and harbor no pangs of sympathy
Because deep down you are wishing you had these problems like me

{ When I was a Kid }

I happily spent a small fortune
A nickel or two at a time
To ride the mechanical horse
That sat in front of the five and dime

I doodled countless hours
Sketched with a pencil and pad
Desperately capturing the essence
My favorite fantasy horses had

I read dozens of their stories
Whenever I found them in books
Stared at hundreds of photos
That portrayed their good looks

On my dresser lived a collection
Of thirty fragile glass figurines
Each one named and treasured
Until way up in my late teens

I knew every cowboy's horse by name
In all those movies and TV shows
I memorized the legendary racers
Who won on the track by a nose

Every spring I entered the contests
With high hopes of winning a foal
Submitting dozens of perfect names
So that I could accomplish my goal

There were times I would lie musing
As I drifted off to sleep on my bed
Thinking of all the questions I'd ask
When I finally got to meet Mr. Ed.

The sounds of nickers and hoofbeats
Filled my thoughts as I looked back
I vividly dreamt Paladin rode in to get me
His clothes and his horse all jet black

Many hours of childhood playtime
Was spent outside running around
While I pretended to be a horse
Rearing and pawing the ground

Those times when my imagination
Would allow me to be the horse
I could actually feel reins pulling
To keep me on course

Other times I would be wild
An untamable and untouchable steed
With wind blowing in my mane
And my spirit being freed

When the annual county fair came around
I would wander the isles of the 4-H barn
Peering into the stalls that housed horses
Wishing it was me who lived on a farm

The only carnival ride I ever ventured
The only other place I could be found
Was on a painted carousel pony
Going rhythmically up and down

If I ever spotted live pony rides
Along the road someplace
You could count on me being there
With a huge grin all over my face

There was a riding stable we'd pass
Enroute to our summer home cabin
My parents always tried to sneak by it
But I couldn't be silenced until they gave in

Then I would ride some poor lifeless pony
Oblivious and alone going around and around
I couldn't explain why it was so important to me
Knowing a small piece of me had been found

Christmas's didn't hold wishes
For baby dolls or Barbies for me
It was that big deluxe farm set
I wanted to see under the tree

I passed time on Sunday afternoon drives
Travelling the country roads of our town
Keeping my eyes glued to the fence lines
Looking for ponies of black, white or brown

When my childhood Easter candy arrived
It wasn't a fancy basket there on the ground
Instead, mine was usually delivered
In a cowgirl hat turned upside down

I can't even count the number
Of different "horses" I made do
Broomsticks, tree limbs, barrels,
Sawhorses and mops to name a few

By the time I was five and already smitten
I was begging to ride but didn't know how
So, although my uncle didn't have a horse
He led me around the farm riding his cow

My cousins had an old farm horse
Who provided us with such fun
We would get on two or three at a time
And through the cornfields we'd go at a run

When it came to the friends I chose
That attended my same school
The best were ones that had horses
It wasn't coincidence - I was no fool

I eagerly awaited those weekends
When I got to stay overnight
Knowing my friend would let me ride
If I played nice and we didn't fight

We didn't take lessons
Our parents didn't insist
We rode bareback with halters
And helmets didn't exist

We learned by "the seat of our pants"
Riding was fast, thrilling and easy
We rode instinctively and fearlessly -
Antics that would now make me queasy

I remember a horseshow at Madison Square
I attended when I had just turned eleven
It was a gift from a family friend who knew
For me, it would be a slice of pure heaven

Although growing up we lived in town
And my pleas for a horse fell on deaf ears
I never gave up hope for a even a minute
Believing wholeheartedly in those tender years

Finally, the long awaited day arrived
Although not until I was full grown
I am proof that wishes do come true
And I got to ride a horse of my own

Now that I'm older and wiser as such
I know that some wishes fell off the grid
But I find I am still dreaming about horses
Not much different than when I was a kid

{ Yep, I Spoil My Horse }

I know it's a subject
Where folks won't agree
But I spoil my horse
To the nth degree

I will give him a treat
Though not out of my hands
I reward him with goodies
When he heeds my commands

And when we are walking
And he gives me a nudge
I laugh at his antics
And don't hold a grudge

When I am stroking his body
I don't make it a quibble
I know it is returning affection
When I get a soft nibble

And when I am brushing him
And his muscles go slack
I don't slap him away
When he grooms me back

When he comes near me
And enters my space
I kiss on his forehead
He knows it's his place

Sometimes my requests
Are met with a goofy glare
I have to laugh out loud
It's a joke that we share

When he gets restless
And his manners may slip
I use a soft voice
Not a kick or a whip

Keeping a horse from eating
Is a fight I don't have to win
Is a mouthful of grass when riding
Really such a terrible sin?

When he shows fear
And maybe just not ready
I don't push him along
Until I feel he is steady

When taking a short break
While we are out on the trail
I am sure to loosen the girth and
Remove the bit without fail

I don't leave him tied
For hours on end
With nothing to eat
Without any friends

He doesn't have to stand
In freezing rain or hot sun
There is always a shelter
Where he can run

I'm too soft you might say
It's only a horse!
I'm used to hearing it -
It's par for the course

But if you think you'll convince me
To be changing my ways
You've got another think coming
Because I know what pays

I know from experience
What a fine friend he can be
If I consider his feelings
He will take care of me

You see there is something
We humans tend to forget
I find it to be true
With most horses I've met

A horse gives up his instincts
His freedom and will
To become what we want
Only trust settles the bill

So, say what you want
My friend has it made
I'll be spoiling my horse
Til the end I'm afraid

{ Conclusion }

I just turned 60 years old this spring and have had a cognizance of my attraction to horses since my eyes could focus and I could point. They have always mesmerized me. I didn't inherit it. I am the only one in a family of 5 children who even likes to be around them, let alone have a passion for riding and caring for them. My siblings and parents preferred living in town near the malls and other conveniences while I longed for the fresh air, natural beauty, open spaces and lots of animals. My childhood years were spent living in the city while dreaming of the country life. Some things you are just born knowing and destiny puts them in your life, eventually, against all odds. The important thing is that I am here now and it is even better than I imagined.

I plan to always have horses in my life in some capacity. I am one of those women who will be perfectly content to sit in the barn on a bale of hay and just listen to them eat and breathe even when I am very, very old. I will always get tremendous pleasure from just looking at them and feeling their presence. I know I am among kindred spirits when I hear silent messages that are not spoken with words but I understand just the same. They are my friends - some of my closest - even though we have our moments when things are not the best between us. It is true that horses don't lie and they force me to take a good hard look in the mirror when we have disagreements of any kind.

It is my life's desire to learn from horses and discover some of those secrets the equine species wants humans to know and understand about them so we can all get along better in this world.

A 93 year old wise and very knowledgeable horseman, the late Bill Dorrance, thought it was important to add a profound statement into the book that he and Leslie Desmond co-wrote titled:"True Horsemanship Through Feel". He wanted to be sure that everyone knew that "Good horsemanship is passed down from one friend to another". In my opinion, he was spot on. The part most people may not realize about that statement is that it is not necessarily between one man or woman and another. I have found more times than not, that one side of that friendship comes from the horse.